W9-AYO-904

FAMOUS AMERICAN INDIAN LEADERS

FOREST DIPLOMAT
The story of Hiawatha

Written by: Jill C. Wheeler
Edited by: Paul J. Deegan

Published by Abdo & Daughters, 6537 Cecilia Circle, Bloomington, Minnesota 55435

Library bound edition distributed by Rockbottom Books, Pentagon Tower, P.O. Box 36036, Minneapolis, Minnesota 55435

Library of Congress Number: 89-084908   ISBN: 0-939179-71-7

Cover and inside illustrations by: Liz Dodson

Hiawatha was hunting. His moccasin-clad feet padded softly over the forest floor, neither cracking a twig nor stirring a leaf. He held his hickory bow tightly to his chest, several antler-tipped arrows clutched in his small brown hand.

The young Iroquois (IHR uh Kwoy) boy stopped suddenly, hearing a low hissing noise in the distance. He ducked behind a tall willow tree to hide until he could see what caused such a strange sound. The hissing grew louder, and Hiawatha thought it sounded like many angry snakes.

Finally, the boy's keen eyes picked up a motion deep within the forest. A thicket of bushes was pushed aside to make room for a tall, dark-skinned man. He looked like Hiawatha's father. But in the man's midnight-black hair were hundreds of hissing, coiling snakes!

Hiawatha sucked in his breath quickly and froze. The snake man continued to walk straight toward him. The hissing grew louder with each step. Hiawatha turned to run, but his feet were like lead. He tripped over the uneven floor of the forest. He lay on his belly. He looked over his shoulder and saw the snake man right behind him.

The man began to bend over. His head of snakes streched toward the Indian boy. The beady eyes of the reptiles flickered...

Hiawatha awoke with a start. It had been just a dream. Still his heart was pounding. His skin was damp with a soft sheen of sweat.

He sat up quickly. His eyes took in the scene of the long house where he lived with his family. It was night. The 10 families living in the long house slept. But the fires still burned in the middle of the bark-covered structure.

Hiawatha's heart had been throbbing loudly in his head. Now it began to quiet. He glanced to his side to see his brothers and sisters and his parents. All slept peacefully on their wooden bunks. He was the only one who had been visited by the evil spirit of the snake man.

The boy took a deep breath and snuggled back under the furs on his pallet. His eyes remained wide open, picking out the rows of vegetables hanging from the high rafters of the long house. It had been a good harvest, and his people, the Onondaga (ahnun DA guh) tribe, would begin celebrating the next day. There would be singing

Hiawatha is visited by the snake man in his dream.

and dancing at the Harvest Festival. Best of all, there would be games. It would be enough to take his mind off the terrible dream.

Thank goodness it was just a dream, Hiawatha thought. But why had he thought of such a man? Surely no man like that could really exist, he thought, drifting back to sleep. Or could he?

The next morning dawned bright and clear in the forest. The time was around the year 1400. It was long before the white man even knew the land of the Iroquois existed. The Indians lived in harmony with nature. They received from the Creator all that they needed or wanted.

Hiawatha was up with the rest of his family at the crack of dawn to prepare for the Harvest Festival. Sleepy families emerged from their long houses and wandered about the walled-in village. The women began to prepare the food for the day's feast, while the men gathered to go hunting. The men met in the center of the village and left through gates in the thick log walls. The walls made each village a small fortress. It was necessary for each tribe to protect itself from other bands of warring Iroquois.

Hiawatha would have liked to have gone hunting with the men, but he was only eight years old — too young to brave the forest. He had heard his uncle, Two Feathers, tell many stories about the dangers lurking in the forest. He knew well of the naked bear. The great beast was covered with smooth, pink skin except for one line of prickly fur down his back. The bear was always on the lookout for Indian children to eat for his supper.

Hiawatha knew what to do should he ever encounter the naked bear. He must wait until the creature lifted its paw, and then shoot an arrow into the tender bottom of his foot. That was where the bear's heart was.

"Hiawatha!" he heard someone shout. Turning toward the center of the village, the boy saw that his uncle was calling him. His face broke into a smile and he raced toward the young man of he was so fond.

"Where are you going, uncle?" Hiawatha asked Two Feathers, his brown eyes wide with curiosity.

"We are going to hunt for meat for the festival," Two Feathers replied. "And what are you going to do today?"

"I'm going hunting, too," Hiawatha replied proudly. "I must test the new bow you made for me. My arrows will fly true to the hearts of many squirrels."

The warriors disappeared through the log wall gates. Hiawatha told his mother he was going hunting with his friend, Running Deer. He grabbed his new bow and a handful of flint-tipped arrows. Then he trotted through the village to find Running Deer.

Like most boys his age, Hiawatha loved to hunt. He only hoped that the snake man would prove to be just a dream.

Hiawatha and Running Deer had a successful morning. Each boy's arrows had found a squirrel. Hiawatha had shot a rabbit as well. They slung their trophies over their shoulders. Then they headed back to camp through the forest.

Young Hiawatha talks to his uncle, Two Feathers.

They were still a long way from the village when Running Deer stopped suddenly. "I'm not ready to return," he said. "The hunters will not have returned, and the feast is not ready yet."

"Yes," Hiawatha said slowly. " What is it you wish to do?"

"We have been hunters this morning," Running Deer said, his eyes bright. "Let us now practice to be warriors!"

"I will pretend to be an Oneida (oh NY duh)," said Running Deer. This was the name of a tribe of enemy Iroquois. "I will let you go ahead of me, and then I will track you. If I cannot find you, you may have my squirrel."

"And if you do find me?" Hiawatha asked.

"Then I get your squirrel," Running Deer said with a laugh. "Come, it will teach us, and your uncle will see that you are eager for his teachings."

Hiawatha consented, and he raced off into the thickness of the forest. Running Deer turned around and closed his eyes. He ran for what seemed like hours. He darted this way and that. He covered his tracks with bushes when he thought they were too easily read.

He stopped short when he came to a tall red willow tree. The red willow had mystical properties, he knew, and he hoped they would aid him in hiding from Running Deer.

Grabbing on to a low limb, he swung up into the tree and began climbing. He would wait there until Running Deer approached. Then he would jump down upon the boy and wrestle him to the ground.

Hiawatha settled himself into a position in the crotch of the tree. He knew he was hidden in the thick leaves high above the ground. All he had to do now was wait.

After a while, he heard the far-off sound of someone approaching. He nearly held his breath to be as quiet as possible so Running Deer would not find him.

But it was not Running Deer who was coming. It was a small band of Indians he did not recognize. Their faces were painted black, red and blue, and they carried javelins and tomahawks.

The band moved almost silently through the woods. Suddenly they stopped underneath Hiawatha's tree. The young boy froze in terror. What would happen if they should find him?

When Iroquois warriors captured their enemies, they either killed them or took them captive.

But it was not Hiawatha for whom the band had stopped. Something was moving through the woods. This had caused them to pause and reach for their weapons. Hiawatha strained his eyes to discover the identity of the stranger, finally catching sight of a familar face. Hiawatha recognized him as Two Feather's friend Lame Wolf. A strangled cry rose up within him as he realized that Lame Wolf was walking straight into the hands of the enemy!

With a shriek, the band of enemy Indians fell upon the lone hunter, their tomahawks slashing in the morning sun. Hiawatha watched for a moment then closed his eyes in terror. Never before had he felt so helpless nor felt such rage.

The battle was over in minutes. Against so many warriors, Lame Wolf never had a chance. As the final insult, the warriors took the hunter's scalp. Then, talking softly among themselves, the group turned and moved away through the forest.

Hiawatha was still. He waited for what seemed like hours. He was afraid to leave the tree because the warriors still might be nearby.

"You have won, Hiawatha," came Running Deer's voice from the forest below him. "I surrender and you may have my kill. Where are..."

Hiawatha saw from his perch that Running Deer had found the hunter's body. The boy's hand moved quickly to his mouth. He began looking around him frantically.

"Running Deer!" Hiawatha called from the tree. "I am up here! I saw it all! It's all right. They are gone," he added as he began to climb down.

The two boys were silent and teary-eyed as they stared at the dead hunter. Then Hiawatha spoke. "We must get back and tell the others," he said.

"But why, uncle? Why did they kill him?" Hiawatha asked later that evening.

"It is a matter of honor," Two Feathers said quietly. "The warriors you saw were Mohawks. A week ago, one of their warriors was killed by Lame Wolf's brother.

"But will not Lame Wolf's family go on the warpath to avenge his death?" Hiawatha asked.

"Yes, already they are planning how," Two Feathers said. "It would be a dishonor to Lame Wolf should his family let his death go unavenged."

"But if they kill one of the Mohawk people, will the Mohawks not come back here and kill again?"

"You are correct, my little one," Two Feather said sadly. "It has been this way since the sun first rose, and it will continue."

"But why?" Hiawatha persisted.

"It is our way. There is no other answer."

Hiawatha was silent. The endless killings made no sense to him. All Indians were brothers, he thought. Why could they not live in peace?

The vision of peace born on that Harvest Festival day continued to haunt Hiawatha. Meanwhile, he grew to manhood under his uncle's watchful eye. He learned the ways of the warpath, and grew strong and brave.

Like the rest of his people, Hiawatha drew figures and symbols to communicate. Hiawatha also devised another way to communicate. The Iroquois people's most valuable articles were beads made from clamshells. These were called wampum.

Each bead took nearly half a day to make. Once made, the beads were woven into belts. Purple wampum beads were the most valuable. But black, white, and shell-colored beads also were valued highly.

Using combinations of the various colors, Hiawatha devised a code so that the deeds of his people would be recorded in the formations of the beads. In such a way, the people's history would be recorded in a form other than the legends and stories which were now passed from generation to generation by mouth.

His people quickly accepted his wampum strings, but Hiawatha's urgings for peace went largely unheard. A few of his people agreed with him but many chiefs still felt that all deaths must be avenged.

One of the chiefs who most strongly opposed Hiawatha was Tadodaho, an Onondaga leader known for his cruelty.

But Hiawatha was patient. Peace was on his side, he thought to himself, he only had to perisit and the people would see the light.

But one day, Hiawatha returned to his village from a trip. Tadodaho's warriors had come while he was away. They had killed Hiawatha's wife and seven daughters.

The great leader was in anguish. His people felt sorry about his loss. However, they refused to rise against Tadodaho for what he had done. In despair, Hiawatha packed up his belongings in a buckskin sack and left the village for good.

He wandered through the forest for many days, stopping finally in the land of the Mohawks to build a lodge of hemlock boughs in a small clearing. If he could not have peace, he would have solitude.

Several moons after Hiawatha had left his village, he was fishing one day when he became aware that he was not alone. He whirled around to look behind him but saw nothing. He began to walk along the lake shore, peering through the thick woods that surrounded the crystal blue waters.

He nearly stumbled upon the canoe before he saw it. Its white sides gleamed in the bright sunshine. He had never seen a canoe made entirely of stone before. Surely, he thought to himself, it did not work. Stones sank in the water — they did not float!

"You admire my canoe," came a voice from behind him. Hiawatha turned to see a tall young man. His white skin shirt and leggings were as brilliant as his canoe. His brown eyes were warm with kindness and understanding. "It has taken me many miles," he said. He was answering Hiawatha's unvoiced question about the stone canoe.

"Who are you?" Hiawatha asked.

"I am called Degandawida," said the man. "I have been looking for you, the one who speaks of peace."

The two returned to Hiawatha's lodge, and Hiawatha fixed his guest some of the fish he had caught. As they ate, Degandawida told Hiawatha of his mission.

"Some years ago, I had a dream, and it has haunted my waking hours ever since," Degandawida explained as he tasted the tender fish. "I saw a giant spruce tree, its strong boughs reaching toward the sky, and at the base, five mighty roots holding fast to the forest floor. At the top of the tree was an eagle, keeping watch. On the floor of the forest was a fresh, white covering of snow."

"The five tribes of the Iroquois," Hiawatha said quietly. "Is that not what you saw in its roots?"

"Indeed it was. And the snow of peace, and the eagle to keep watch for those who might destroy that peace. How is it that you can read my dreams?"

"Because I have had the same dream," Hiawatha said slowly. "Mine has not come at night, but in

Hiawatha admires the stone canoe.

the living of many days, seeing the evils of war and hatred and killing."

"Then you will help me?" Degandawida asked gently.

"What is it you need of me?" Hiawatha replied.

"Already I have spoken with your Mohawk brothers, and they seem eager for peace," Degandawida said. "I need you to convince the Onondagas to lay down their weapons. It will be a difficult task, for Tadodaho still rules with an evil hand."

"Will you help me?" Degandawida asked again.

"I will do whatever I can," Hiawatha answered.

For many moons thereafter, Hiawatha and Degandawida traveled the forest. They spoke peace to whomever would listen.

They spoke of a league of tribes. It would be governed by a council of 50 chiefs. The chiefs would be selected by the women of the tribes.

"The chiefs," Hiawatha told the people, "must have hearts closed to anger, hate and criticism. Their hearts must be filled with peace and good will. Their minds must be eager to soak up the welfare of their people like a gentle spring rain."

The chiefs, they stressed, could not be warriors, for there were war chiefs to handle matters such as that. And if a council member were to kill another person the killer would be barred from the council. This would be done even if the killing had been in self defense.

Crowds of Mohawks, Senecas (SEN un kahs), Cayugas (kah YOO gahs), Oneidas and Hiawatha's own people, the Onondagas, gathered to hear the message of the two great speakers. As they listened, they nodded and spoke among themselves about the foolishness of their warring ways.

However, the true test of the two men's message of peace came one day when they spoke to the people of Hiawatha's great enemy, Tadodaho.

"Think not of yourselves, nor of your own generation," Degandawida told the gathering. "Think of continuing generations of our families,

think of our grandchildren and of those yet unborn, whose faces are coming from beneath the ground."

"It is time to lay down our tomahawks and let a great binding law lead us down the pathway to peace," Hiawatha added.

"And what law do you suggest?" came a question from the crowd.

"We suggest that the People of the Longhouse adopt new ways," Degandawida said. "These ways will bring health of mind and body, and peace among all. Under the new way you will respect the rights of each man. You will see that justice is done for all. You will defend each other against wrong. You will seek the power of the Great Spirit."

The crowd murmured excitedly at the prospect. To have peace at last! They could live free of the fear of lightning-swift morning raids. There would be no more bloodshed for bloodshed. The idea was welcomed — by most.

Hiawatha and Degandawida exchanged glances as the people left them. Things had gone well.

Hiawatha speaks to the tribes about his plan for peace.

"You who speak of alliance," came a rough voice from in front of them. "You are but cowards hiding in the robes of peace."

Hiawatha saw that Tadodaho had been among the crowd and remained. Hiawatha decided that like any other man, Tadodaho could be persuaded.

"Come," Hiawatha told him. "Let us talk."

Tadodaho stared at him warily. He did not trust this man who spoke of peace. This man wanted to destroy all the traditions of the Iroquois people. What if his people should agree to this Great Peace, Tadodaho was thinking. Surely other Indians then would think of his people as cowards.

"We will talk," Tadodaho said finally. "But your breath will be of no use."

After many hours of talking and singing, Hiawatha was able to soften Tadodaho's heart towards peace. Tadodaho also was chosen to tend the Iroquois League's central fire. It would burn as an eternal flame representing the Great Peace.

The time came for the first meeting of the League's ruling Council. All 50 chiefs had been selected by their tribes. They gathered in a circle on the shore of a lake in the land of the Onondaga. Each chief wore deer antlers to signify their membership in the council. They would hold the membership for life.

A fire burned brightly in the center of the circle. Its flames illuminated Degandawida's white figure as he stood to address the gathering.

In his hand, Degandawida held a slender white pine sapling. He held it high above his head as he spoke.

"This is the Tree of Peace," he said. "This, is our nation."

Degandawida laid the sapling on the ground, and bending down, he began to dig. He dug in the earth with a stick until he had scraped out a hole. He then reached into his belt and withdrew his tomahawk, dropping it into the hole.

"Now, we bury our weapons. No more will brother rise against brother to shed blood on the forest floor," he said solemnly.

Picking up the sapling, he shook the dirt from its roots. He held it high saying, "These four roots are the roots of our peace. They stretch toward the east, the north, the west, and the south. They spread and provide nourishment to the tree. So shall our peace spread through the nation and strengthen our people."

The 50 chiefs were silent as Degandawida planted the tiny pine. Carefully he stamped the earth around it. "If any man outside the Iroquois desires the Great Peace, he may follow the roots to their source," he said. "All who seek peace are welcome to take shelter beneath the tree."

Next, Hiawatha spoke, outlining the rules of the great law which would bind them as a nation. First and foremost, there would be no killing for revenge, he said. Those who broke the law and murdered must pay the victim's family for their loss.

Hiawatha continued to explain the laws of the peace, each one carefully measured to ensure justice, truth and freedom. The chiefs listened

The central fire where all the tribes leaders gathered.

silently, memorizing his words to take back to their people.

The Council would meet at least once every five years. It would meet in the chief Onondaga village, he said. More meetings would be called should any important questions arise.

The Mohawks were Keepers of the Eastern Door. The Senecas were Keepers of the Western Door. They would sit on the east side of the fire. They would be the first to discuss any questions. When they arrived at a decision, they would throw the question across the central fire to the Oneidas and Cayugas. They would sit on the west.

What if the two sides did not reach the same decision, the chiefs asked. The Onondagas were the Keepers of the Central Fire, Hiawatha said. They would be seated at the north of the fire to help the two sides agree. When all agreed on a decision, it would stand as the word of the League.

Finally, Hiawatha held up a wampum belt. He had woven it to tell of the Great Peace and the people who had sworn to uphold it. He turned to show it to Degandawida. But the man was nowhere in sight. Hiawatha walked quickly out of the lodge to the shore of the lake to look for him.

In the distance, he thought he could see a glimmer of a white canoe in the moonlight. But the glimmer soon disappeared, and Degandawida failed to return.

Hiawatha never saw his friend again.

The Iroquois nation now was as one. However, Hiawatha felt there still was more work to be done. Gathering up his few possessions, he took to the forest trails. He would spread the word of the Great Peace to other Indian nations.

No more were his words of peace greeted with scorn and mistrust. Many other tribes, from the Tuscaroras to the Delawares to the Shawnees listened intently to the great speaker's words and then joined the League. Those tribes who resisted membership in the League found themselves faced with an army of League warriors, who would kill if need be to win another tribe into the alliance. Soon the influence of the Great Peace stretched from the Atlantic Ocean to the Mississippi River and from Canada to what was to become the Carolinas.

When the League had grown strong, the now elderly Hiawatha turned to another venture. He began to build roads. He called upon the help of many strong braves. They would clear existing Iroquois paths of brush and trees.

By the time Hiawatha drew his last breath, tribes who had once been rivals now worked together, and hundreds of brightly colored wampum belts told the tale of the Great Peace and the eternal flame. Thanks to Hiawatha's efforts, the Five Nations of the Iroquois grew to be the greatest and most influential Indian nation in the history of North America.

James Madison pushed his chair back from the huge mahogany desk and laid his head in his hands. He was only 36 years old, but his task in the summer of 1787 was a huge one. He was writing a constitution for the newly formed United States of America.

"What troubles you, James," said his elderly friend, Benjamin Franklin. Franklin was sitting near a window, looking out on to the streets of Philadelphia.

"You know my feelings on government by the people and for the people," Madison said finally. "You also know how the rest of the Continental Congress feels about my ideas."

"They do not believe the people are fit to govern themselves," Franklin said. "It is your duty to convince them."

"But how?" Madison asked. "True democracy exists in ancient history and in the minds of philosophers. It has been tried here recently, but only among small groups. I need a modern example. I need an example of an entire nation so I can prove to them that it works!"

"You have one," Franklin said quietly. "Do you not remember your trip three years ago when you accompanied the Marquis de Lafayette?"

"Yes, but..."

"And you saw the Iroquois people?" Franklin probed gently.

"The Great Law of Peace," Madison said softly, remembering. "The Iroquois League!"

"Indeed, a modern confederacy of sovereign nations represented at a central council," Franklin continued. "With laws guarding freedom of speech and individual rights. The very system of government you desire."

Franklin pulled out his pocket watch and glanced at the time. "I must take my leave now, friend," he said. Rising to his feet, he wobbled toward the door.

Madison sat silently after the door latched behind his friend. Dipping his quill pen in the ink jar, he began to write.

If the will of the majority cannot be trusted where there are diversified and conflicting interests, it can be trusted nowhere.